CW00391241

SKY MALL

Eric Kocher

Rattle | *Studio City, California* | 2024

Rattle Foundation
12411 Ventura Blvd
Studio City, CA 91604
www.rattle.com

CONTENTS

ACKNOWLEDGMENTS

Thank you to my family, Audrey, Louise, and Oscar, for making a space for me to write these poems. And thank you to Alan Rossi, Patrick Whitfill, and Andrew Dally for helping me see them clearly.

I'm particularly grateful to Sam Amadon and Liz Countryman for being such generous editors and friends. I'm not sure if I would write any poems if not for the encouragement from Brian Trimboli, Florencia Varela, and Laura-Eve Engel—thank you.

Of course, thank you to Tim Green and everyone at *Rattle* for bringing these poems into the world. And thank you to Steve Snell for the artwork on the cover.

The poem "Sky Mall" was first published in issue 9 of *Oversound*.

SKY MALL

Sky Mall

Among clouds, I have a Dewar's.
I'm going to Connecticut.

My wife and daughter are already there
And our apartness feels material.

I am paying very close attention
And compiling a record of disclosure,

Trying to be mindful of the many
Arrivals and departures

In which I am entangled,
which entangle me.

Although, above me, someone's luggage
Is a mystery, so full of items.

I really don't want to cry on this plane.
I want to say that I am having a nice time.

Other people seem angry at the plane,
Angry to be traveling in general.

But you are always traveling,
I want to tell them,

You are always going somewhere.
Wait, where is the earth?

I just see sky.
I've never seen it in quite this way.

Blue, yes, of course, blue,
But also trying not to be, almost aware

[...]

Of its blueness as a lie,
An emergent property that suggests

A point-of-view overcompensating
For its needing to move on.

The plane levels,
But I worry I'll keep looking up forever.

I've already seen it.
Just the other day, NASA released new

Photos of the universe.
These are the oldest galaxies, they said,

But the oldest galaxies looked just like
The new ones.

They just look like tiny things
You want to pinch between your fingers.

Oh, right, the world is here.
It seems to be made of lines.

At least some of it is made of plane,
Which isn't really a substance as much as it is

A stand-in for many substances coming together,
Whose togetherness appears to us as plane.

I think it's strange that our apartness
Is composed partially of what will bring us

Together, that our togetherness, like being
Apart, is also composed, is itself a composure.

After my daughter was born, I learned
How to miss someone in real time.

I would look at her and think,
I am missing you,

Even though she was right there,
I wanted to be even more right there.

I kept wanting to smush our faces together,
Although I wasn't really sure

Of what that would accomplish or mean.
It was just this helpless

And obvious wanting to eliminate
Any distance between us

Without any deference for interiority
And its invention of between.

Ok, we are coming up on a big cloud.
I want to describe it to you:

It's quite tall, and the top of it seems
To be trying to leave the rest of the cloud,

But it can't.
It's like it's made from a different kind

Of cloud material, a bit wispier,
Like it was made by a barista.

I wonder if my impulse to see a cloud
In terms of labor production

Demonstrates the completeness
With which I have internalized and accepted

The commodification of matter on an atomic level.
I'm sorry.

[...]

9

I stopped paying attention and now
The cloud is gone

In the sense it is no longer in the frame
My small window offers.

I wanted to tell you more about the cloud's
Many details and properties,

It's topography and textures,
How it suggests a realness more real

Than we often give credence to,
That we must pry back from the sublime.

Even though the memory is fresh,
If I close my eyes, it's like I can still see it,

Describing a memory is describing
A different perceptual function,

And while my memory is a thing,
It would require me to describe

Multiple layers of time, one on top
Of another, like listening to two songs

At once, one, frenetic and jazzy,
Swinging wildly between time changes

And keys,
The other, a sweet folk tune

About someone doing their best,
Just trying to see their family.

Here's a little secret:
Time is passing for us in different ways.

There were snacks, a second Dewar's,
Some chitchat with this lady from Connecticut

Sitting next to me, this whole other person
Who has had three chardonnays.

I thought about my daughter.
I thought about my wife.

I had a thought that was something like,
Wow, we are all the way up here.

How often do we get to change our perspective
This completely?

The last time I checked people couldn't
Third person themselves,

Or turn into mantis shrimp.
I say mantis shrimp because I think

They are the kind of shrimp that can see
A lot of colors.

At least more colors than we can.
More colors than we can even understand.

This is complicated because our talking about
Things requires an acknowledgement

Of their properties,
But our understanding of their properties

Is incomplete.
I couldn't explain much to a mantis shrimp.

We would get stuck describing
Distance to each other.

[...]

The shrimp would be trying to tell me about
The infinite refractions inside of something gray

And I would be apologizing
About so much plastic.

I could ask the shrimp if it's ever visited
The Great Pacific Garbage Patch,

Which, to my understanding, is sort of like
The holy gathering of things

Determined to be no longer of use
To us and thereby discarded,

Which, when considered from the perspective
Of the things, taking into account

Something like their autonomy,
Could be seen as a stay against loneliness,

A communion of being
Without only being for.

Ok, now it looks like we are over Antarctica.
There's just this one huge cloud going on forever.

It is very flat, very homogenous.
It might be the world's biggest cloud.

Beneath me there must be thousands of people
Thinking that it's a cloudy day,

But they don't even know the extent
To which that is true.

They can only see a very small part of the cloud.
Maybe they think it is just over them?

Like one of those cartoons where the cloud
Follows one person and rains only on them.

Maybe beneath me there are a thousand people
Feeling self-pity?

I recognize that there are important things,
Narrative elements, that are missing.

You might be wondering why I am apart
From my family, why they are in Connecticut

And I am flying there with a Dewar's.
You might be wondering if this pivot

Back to myself might have something to do
With self-pity.

The truth is that it's hard to explain.
It's complicated and painful,

But the details don't belong to me.
The details are the whole thing.

The details enact the composure of it.
Each one of them is very important,

But there are just way too many of them.
They are both numerous, infinite,

And utterly unique and singular.
I think if you think about your own details,

You'll get the general idea
Of what I am saying.

One detail that I will share, however,
Because now I feel like I owe you some context,

[...]

Is that I was on the phone with our insurance agent
Because our car was hit while parked

In front of our house,
And I had to say to our insurance agent

That I was sorry,
There was a family emergency and I had to go.

Someone was gone, or almost gone,
And it required a spreading out

Of our bodies, a momentary redistribution
In which our family must expand

And contract like a lung,
Like everything else in the universe,

Or at least that seems to be the implication
Of the photographs from NASA.

I worry I've committed to making a catalogue of things,
Strange and wonderful, terrifying and sad.

In this case, that I had to go was a thing.
Now, the sky is.

The world, down there, is very much a thing,
A pretty silly thing to have been made like this.

Look at these silly little roads,
Developments that are shaped like kidneys.

Some places, from this point of view,
Seem like they could be anywhere,

But they are not anywhere.
That requires an obfuscation of detail,

A willingness to ignore the absence of.
Earlier in the flight, when I ordered a Dewar's,

The woman beside me,
The woman from Connecticut,

Told me that her husband used to drink Dewar's
When they would fly, so now she felt

Like she was flying with her husband.
I wanted to ask her if it would have been nice

For me to pretend that I was him.
I could say things like, I love you,

And, yes, dear.
I didn't say that, though.

I'm not sure what I said.
I think I said, that's nice, and raised my Dewar's

in her direction.
I think I also did a little thing with my eyebrows.

Something to suggest that I understood,
I was empathetic, but, also, that I wasn't

Going to dig any deeper, I wasn't going to
Pick at the suggestion

That he was, in some way, gone.
I was having a hard time already

With that concept and, in particular,
Trying to understand my own goneness,

And the eventual goneness of the people
That I loved most.

[...]

I thought that maybe I should touch
Her hand slightly with my hand,

Almost by accident,
Like the smallest version of smushing

Our faces together,
With real face smushing being obviously

Off the table, but I wanted
Some way of saying that I am here

And that she is here,
And whether or not I am her husband

Or my wife's husband,
That we, too, are things, that we take up

Space, or rather, are space
Taking up itself,

Tending to itself and to the spaces
We get to care for,

For whatever time our space
Is materialized as this.

I was having a hard time thinking
About my daughter thinking about me

As gone, which is almost certainly
Something she will have to think,

That it was possible she was already
Thinking some variation of.

Which is why I didn't ask about her husband,
Which is why I did the thing with my eyebrows

That didn't mean anything specific.
Ok, we are coming up on New York.

That means we are getting close.
I find myself thinking of the names of bridges.

The plane banks right and is headed east
Over Long Island, which is where I am from.

We are passing over my childhood now.
We are passing over my memories.

I am having a lot of feelings about a highway
I didn't know I could have.

I used to be sad on one when I went to work
At a Borders Bookstore in two thousand and seven.

I didn't know where my life would go then
But I had a lot of questions and a lot of expectations.

I didn't know my wife or daughter existed,
But I wanted them to.

Or at least I wanted to feel
How I thought the hypothetical versions of them

Might make me feel.
My wanting was something separate from them,

But they were very real.
My wife was somewhere else,

Probably Connecticut,
Probably where I am going,

Where, it turns out, I had always been going,
Only unable to see that then.

[...]

I was too busy being sad
on the Meadowbrook Parkway listening to CDs.

Even though my daughter wasn't born,
The material of her being was here,

It was just on its way to being her,
Some of it being sad on the Meadowbrook Parkway,

Unaware that the sadness had to travel backwards
From this moment, flying on a plane,

To be fully understood, to be able to become someone.
It was future sadness.

Maybe feelings move between cracks in spacetime,
That each felt thing is literally cosmic,

Is the universe trying to compose itself,
Bringing each piece back together,

Like the whole Big Bang thing was a mistake
We are trying to undo.

There's gravity, after all, the pull
Every single thing has on every other.

There's how you feel it pulling you.
Maybe that's what this is, all of it,

My being sad, my being on a plane,
The Dewar's, the woman from Connecticut,

Connecticut itself, everything you've ever felt
Or seen or touched, and everything

You haven't, it's all just trying to remember
How to put itself back together,

How it once was one thing and only one thing.
Sometimes, a thing is a shape

That slowly gets filled in with details
And becomes impossible to describe.

Now, when we land, I will see my family.
They are coming to pick me up.

They have been traveling towards me
While I traveled towards them.

The plane traveling down towards the planet
And the planet traveling up towards the plane.

The trees and the houses and the highways
Getting closer, acquiring details

Like everything is making itself
Less categorical, less a stand-in for

And just allowed to be exactly as it is.
When I see my family

I will say that I wrote a poem on the plane,
That I thought it was about travel,

But it wasn't, it was about them.
What's that thing people say, something

About the journey, that the journey matters
More than where you are going?

No, I don't think that's true.
The plane has to land on something.

Good News

If you liked where we've been headed,
I have good news for you,

This is going to be just like it,
Except for in a few important ways.

This time we will also begin with a Dewar's,
Also on a plane,

But now there's a completely different vibe
With noise-canceling headphones

Supplying a playlist I made a few years ago,
Downloaded, and forgot about.

It has all the hits
I was into then.

This plane, for reference, is flying
In the next calendar year,

The summer after the last one,
And is currently way above the flattest part of

The middle of America,
Where the world is farmed into corners.

According to sources,
We are headed northwest towards Seattle,

My wife and me, where we will rent a car
To drive to a ferry to stay on an island to go on a boat

To see whales, to hike in a forest of enormous trees,
To rediscover lost parts of ourselves

And each other, all the while
Saying that we are on vacation,

Taking a much-needed break from
The ordinariness of our lives.

What we mean by this is that we are taking
A break from being parents, sort of,

Outsourcing the labor of it to other family,
But continuing to let the simple fact of it,

That our daughter exists,
Shape every facet of our being, of what

We say and don't say, what we do
And don't do.

I should probably add that, because of this,
If you liked where we were headed,

This will probably also be disappointing
Because things are going to be different

This time, as we are headed not towards
Something but away from it,

Trying to create distance
Instead of erase it,

Which suggests that this will be full
Of glaring and obvious gaps.

In fact, I'm planning to bypass
The artifice of continuity altogether

And try to unfold with the unfolding of things,
Relaxing into them with my seat slightly reclined.

[...]

For the moment, let's just appreciate a few things:
First, that my wife is here with me this time,

That our togetherness is a part of the distance
We are pretending we are making

By saying hello, yes, welcome, etc. to the opening
Of space before us.

Second, it seems worth pointing out,
That the woman in the middle seat in the row

Ahead of us, has earrings that say something,
Her name, maybe, in cursive,

And with her candy red hair, she is dancing
To whatever is in her headphones,

Not seeming to notice or care
If anyone around her minds.

I would like to think that maybe
We are in cahoots together,

That we are ready to begin a new journey
With the simple premise that we are having a good time.

Safety Features

Among clouds, I have an empty plastic cup
But I'm afraid where we are going,

The Pacific Northwest,
The Cascadia Subduction Zone,

Will be struck by a massive and violent
Earthquake that erases everything west

Of I-5, that my wife and I
Will be tragically killed by a tsunami

While on a whale-watching tour,
Clumsy in the romantic wonder

Of nature, and that our daughter
Will have to learn what that means

In age-appropriate chunks as she gets older,
First that we are gone, then how,

That we were people who were clumsy
In our romantic wonder of nature,

And so on like that until I am breathing
All weird and panicking up here,

Trying to remind myself that none of this
Is an appropriate disposition

For someone going on vacation. At least
I can be grateful that we all know what to do

In the event of a water landing.
We know about the safety features,

[...]

Of this particular aircraft,
Even as I feel my feet swelling in the atmosphere.

I untie my shoes and press the button overhead.
I'll get another Dewar's; I'll try this again.

Flight Test

Now that we are over mountains,
We want to know which mountains,

But their names are impossible to know.
My best guess is The Mountains of Wyoming,

Which is not their formal name,
But if imbued with enough formality,

Say, in a story, later, or here in this poem,
One might be willing to accept it as sufficient

Without needing to fully unpack
My relationship with geography. Although,

Note to self: I should take some time to unpack
My relationship with geography.

Maybe that can be another poem
Where I try to reimagine everything

Cartographically, with the reductive
Clarity of two-dimensions?

Right now, I would just like to pay attention
To things unfolding before me. After all,

We are here because we need to relax,
To take a break from being a routine-person,

A grocery store-person, an email-person,
A person who needs to clean out the gutters,

Stain the deck, a person with an inferiority complex
Who isn't very good at making phone calls.

[...]

25

No, we are here to have a good time,
To enjoy the free in-flight entertainment.

Cocaine Bear

Everything, as far as I can tell, is about motherhood
In some way, and this is, eventually, gratuitously so,

A reminder, maybe, needing forgiveness,
That is also worth forgiving.

My wife is watching a show about a lawyer,
I think, who is also good at surfing.

Good for him.
But that is based only on a few quick glances

Away from my own study
Of the horrifying cruelty of nature

As portrayed through the continual dismemberment
Of characters who both do and do not deserve it.

My wife takes her motherhood with her.
There's no such thing as making distance from that.

Another mother on the plane
Is pacing up and down the aisle with her infant.

You can tell that their moment is fragile
By her face and the faces of the people around them.

I remember our version of this was not
So long ago, but elsewhere, in another sky.

I understand that if someone woke her child,
The details of how she might tear all of us apart.

Strong Suit

Ok, the flight is almost over, and I am realizing
That this time can't be like the last time

Which was mostly about being contained,
That this time I have to open myself in some way.

I have to be better at being open to new things
And recognizing them as they are happening,

Even if I don't know what they are just yet,
Which, I suppose, is what makes them new.

Anyone who knows me knows this
Isn't my strong suit, that I have never been

Particularly good at going with the flow.
I am more so the type of person

Who complicates the flow for other people,
Who finds it necessary to point out

All the things that make the flow impossible
To achieve or maintain.

I suppose that's one nice thing about planes,
That I am strapped in up here, paid good money to be,

And there's nothing I can do or say
Within reason to change my going or not

Going with the flow,
That the flow is an unstoppable thing,

Composed of an unstoppable sequence of flowing,
One mounting on top of another in endless frames,

And I am merely a passenger, here,
Over-complicating the ride.

Passenger Deck

Now we are on the ferry we flew to drive to,
It's enormous engines vibrating

Every molecule, spreading out,
A family of ducks getting out of the way.

My wife claims there are fish jumping,
But every time I look up

They are gone, or she is lying.
I have become suspicious of my pursuit

Of remoteness, of seeking out places far away
And difficult to get to,

Places with fewer people, more trees.
I am suspicious

Because I know it's at least somewhat
Insincere, that I very deeply need other people

Around me to feel safe, to feel important,
That part of my departure is the performance

Of departure, the making of the image of one.
This departure is certainly

Not about being alone.
My wife and I are here as a way of being

Even more together than we normally are,
Or maybe being together

In a way that we used to be all the time
Before our daughter was born.

Her birth made us closer, for sure,
It made our little story seem

Impossibly big and important,
Like we were conducting the soundtrack

To our daughter's grand entrance
To being with other people, to being with herself.

But it also made certain parts of ourselves
And each other seem far away,

Like one of those distant places
I am always interested in going.

I tell my wife that, of all the places
On the planet, the place I want most to be

Is the North Pole, that I feel the Arctic calling me
As if from inside of a dream.

A smaller boat passes by and I'm surprised
When we are unmoved

By its little wake, that the waves,
Regardless of their size,

Should rock us, however gently.
But now we are on this gigantic boat

Looking for those people we used to be,
Trying to remember them without erasing

Each other, without erasing
The people that they have become

And all the ways they are growing still.
We also came here looking for whales,

[...]

I should add, that we bought tickets from people
Who promised we would see them.

And now that we are out here looking
For ourselves among them,

I have no idea why. Or, maybe,
I'm worried what might happen if they see me.

Seeing Whales

The guide says there's a correlation between cruelty
And intelligence, as the pod of killer whales

Surrounds a small group of harbor seals
Warming in the sun on a rocky outcrop.

This pod, the guide explained, is transient,
Covers vast distances, and has learned how to scare

The seals by slapping their tails
Against the surface of the water.

If we are lucky, he says, we might see them
Toss a seal into the air to stun it before taking it

Apart, first removing its skin, then choosing
Its heart and liver, before discarding the other

Less nutrient dense organs.
You see, he says, you have to remember

That these are acoustic beings.
Their world is made of sound.

So as the seals panic and dive into the water,
The whales can hear the quickened beating

Of their hearts, that their understanding
Of the world includes everything that goes on inside it.

Mountain Lake

The next day I wake up and my wife
Is coming into the hotel room

And the first thing she tells me is that she found
A secret garden, which are her actual words,

Where she sat and absorbed as much sunlight
As she could, and then the second thing

She tells me is that she is pregnant, again,
That assuming nothing goes wrong,

Our daughter, who is on the other side
Of the country, is going to be a big sister.

I say I think I am still dreaming, probably,
But not in that cliché sense

Of life being somehow hazy or surreal,
But rather that words she is saying,

The order of them, seem more like something
Someone would say in a dream,

Especially the secret garden thing,
But minus me now saying

That I felt like I was dreaming,
Which is a near guarantee that I am awake.

As we say this, I realize I had already known
On some level but I had been trying to pretend

Like I didn't know, partly because I didn't want
To get my hopes up,

And partly because I knew that when I actually knew it,
When I knew it for real

It would lead me to knowing
Too many other things,

And then, when we knew it together, when we started
Saying it out loud, the meanings would snowball

Into bigger meanings, and then we would
Have to start making real decisions. First,

We decide the best thing to do with this new
Information is to go for a hike, as we had planned,

So, we drive to a trail called Mountain Lake
Which, we agreed, are two of the best

Geological features, independent of each other,
So what better place could we be without compromise.

After we decide this, all around us
Are these dizzyingly old trees,

western redcedar, Douglas fir, western hemlock,
All climbing one, two hundred feet

Into the air, and the air itself so very quiet,
Soft almost, making space for whatever

We have to say, which is a lot, so we say everything
We can, starting with the obvious stuff

Like who we think this new person might be,
What we might call them,

How tired everyone is going to be again,
Before moving onto the other stuff,

[…]

The fragility of it all, how the little patterns
We've managed to summon will change,

That our daughter's world
Will simultaneously expand forever

And collapse inward, both a new galaxy
And a black hole, and that neither of us

Know how to say any of this to her.
Beside us, we can't decide if the lake

Is green or blue, nor what determines
The greenness or blueness of any given lake.

Its chemical composition, maybe,
The algae and other organisms living in the lake,

Their eating and shitting
And synthesizing each other, maybe,

The trees blanketing the surrounding mountains,
How the light is refracting and diffusing

Among them reciprocally, maybe,
Some or none or all of these things together.

The guide on the whale-watching tour
Explained that orcas live in matriarchal

Societies, that they are among the few other
Beings on the planet who experience menopause,

Which is important because it creates space
For matriarch to teach the new mothers

And their babies how to hunt and play and be.
Explained this way, everything seems very clear,

As if we live within some order or logic that permeates
The way that life unfolds, like we are surrounded

Always by helpful explanations
Of what it is we are doing here,

If only we have the time and attention
To understand them.

When I ask my wife what kind of matriarch
She wants to be, she says a fancy one

Who surrounds herself with fancy things.
I know that this isn't what she means,

But for a moment I feel very fancy, or that maybe
I might one day be a fancier version of myself.

The forest seems fancier, now,
And the quiet air, and the mountain, and the lake.

And I remember this pattern, too,
That a small thing can radiate outward, change

Everything around it.
My wife touches her hand to her stomach

And says that this trip was supposed to be her break
From being a parent,

And we keep climbing up along the ridge
Until somewhere below us

Is that other life we lived, so small now
That it must have always been gone.

Red-Eye Home

Among clouds, I'm without a time zone,
Let loose from the constraints of keeping track.

There's only night, now, and a hundred of us
Or more uncomfortably sleeping, or wanting sleep,

Dreaming up a place far above the place we live.
With each moment, all of us becoming so different

It will be like we are arriving someplace new,
Alien to everything, changed so completely

We'll need to reintroduce ourselves
To the planet when we land.

ABOUT THE RATTLE CHAPBOOK SERIES

The Rattle Chapbook Series publishes and distributes a chapbook to all of *Rattle*'s print subscribers along with each quarterly issue of the magazine. Most selections are made through the annual Rattle Chapbook Prize competition (deadline: January 15th). For more information, and to order other chapbooks from the series, visit our website.

www.R a t t l e.com/*chapbooks*